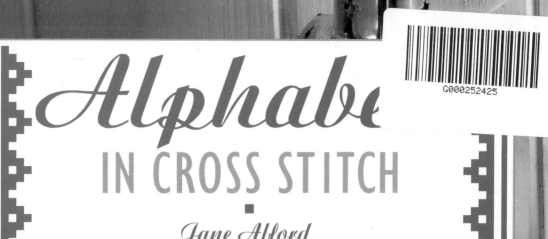

Alphabet
IN CROSS STITCH

Jane Alford

G000252425

MEREHURST

THREADS
The projects in this book were all stitched with DMC stranded cotton
embroidery threads. The keys given with each chart also list thread
combinations for those who wish to use Anchor or Madeira threads.
It should be pointed out that the shades produced by different
companies vary slightly, and it is not always possible to find
identical colours in a different range.

THE CHARTS
Some of the designs in this book are very detailed and due to
inevitable space limitations, the charts may be shown on a
comparatively small scale; in such cases, readers may find it
helpful to have the particular chart with which they are
currently working enlarged.

Published in 1994 by Merehurst Limited
Ferry House, 51-57 Lacy Road, Putney, London SW15 1PR
© Copyright 1994 Merehurst Limited
ISBN 1 85391 377 4
Reprinted 1995, 1996

A catalogue record for this book is available from the British Library.

Managing Editor Heather Dewhurst
Edited by Diana Lodge
Designed by Maggie Aldred
Photography by Marie-Louise Avery
Illustrations by John Hutchinson
Typesetting by BMD Graphics, Hemel Hempstead
Colour separation by Fotographics Limited, UK – Hong Kong
Printed in Hong Kong

*Merehurst is the leading publisher of craft books and has an excellent range
of titles to suit all levels. Please send to the address above for our
free catalogue, stating the title of this book.*

CONTENTS

ℐNTRODUCTION

Since the earliest times, embroiderers have used their skills to add decorative personal touches to clothes, table and bed linen and samplers. Sometimes an item might be embellished with a symbol associated with a particular individual, such as the Napoleonic bee, but more often it would be the name or initials of the maker or recipient.

A sampler, for example, was made to provide a record of stitches and patterns worked in embroidery, and acted as a reference for the needlewoman's future projects. Decorative alphabets were included with the stitches, patterns and traditional motifs. The name, date and age of the embroiderer were often added – frequently only to be unpicked years later, when the maker reached a certain age.

Cross stitch is one of the oldest, and simplest, of all embroidery stitches. With the help of the instructions on this and the following pages, even complete beginners will find that they are able to select letters from the delightful decorative alphabets to be found in this book, using them to decorate a wide range of items in order to make highly personal and treasured gifts.

The book finishes with two beautiful samplers – one modern in style and one traditional – for those who enjoy exercising and displaying their embroidery skills.

Whatever you choose to embellish with cross stitching, you will surely find a suitable alphabet in this book.

ℬASIC SKILLS

■

BEFORE YOU BEGIN

PREPARING THE FABRIC

Even with an average amount of handling, many evenweave fabrics tend to fray at the edges, so it is a good idea to overcast the raw edges, using ordinary sewing thread, before you begin.

THE INSTRUCTIONS

Each project begins with a full list of the materials that you will require. All the designs are worked on evenweave fabrics such as Aida, produced by Zweigart. The measurements given for the embroidery fabric include a minimum of 5cm (2in) all around to allow for stretching it in a frame and preparing the edges to prevent them from fraying.

Colour keys for stranded embroidery cottons – DMC, Anchor or Madeira – are given with each chart. It is assumed that you will need to buy one skein of each colour mentioned in a particular key, even though you may use less, but where two or more skeins are needed, this information is included in the main list of requirements.

To work from the charts, particularly those where several symbols are used in close proximity, some readers may find it helpful to have the chart enlarged so that the squares and symbols can be seen more easily. Many photocopying services will do this for a minimum charge.

Before you begin to embroider, always mark the centre of the design with two lines of basting stitches, one vertical and one horizontal, running from edge to edge of the fabric, as indicated by the arrows on the charts.

As you stitch, use the centre lines given on the chart and the basting threads on your fabric as reference points for counting the squares and threads to position your design accurately.

WORKING IN A HOOP

A hoop is the most popular frame for use with small areas of embroidery. It consists of two rings, one fitted inside the other; the outer ring usually has an adjustable screw attachment so that it can be tightened to hold the stretched fabric in place.

Hoops are available in several sizes, ranging from 10cm (4in) in diameter to quilting hoops with a diameter of 38cm (15in). Hoops with table stands or floor stands attached are also available.

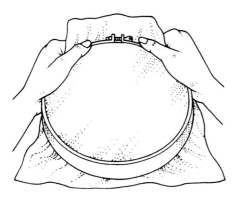

1 To stretch your fabric in a hoop, place the area to be embroidered over the inner ring and press the outer ring over it, with the tension screw released. Tissue paper can be placed between the outer ring and the embroidery, so that the hoop does not mark the fabric. Lay the tissue paper over the fabric when you set it in the hoop, then tear away the central embroidery area.

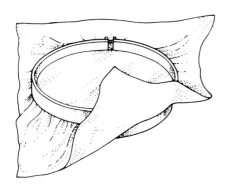

2 Smooth the fabric and, if necessary, straighten the grain before tightening the screw. The fabric should be evenly stretched.

WORKING IN A RECTANGULAR FRAME

Rectangular frames are more suitable for larger pieces of embroidery. They consist of two rollers, with tapes attached, and two flat side pieces, which slot into the rollers and are held in place by pegs or screw attachments. Available in different sizes, either alone or with adjustable table or floor stands, frames are measured by the length of the roller

tape, and range in size from 30cm (12in) to 68cm (27in).

As alternatives to a slate frame, canvas stretchers and the backs of old picture frames can be used. Provided there is sufficient extra fabric around the finished size of the embroidery, the edges can be turned under and simply attached with drawing pins (thumb tacks) or staples.

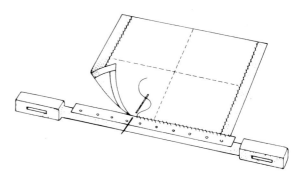

1 To stretch your fabric in a rectangular frame, cut out the fabric, allowing at least an extra 5cm (2in) all around the finished size of the embroidery. Baste a single 12mm (½in) turning on the top and bottom edges and oversew strong tape, 2.5cm (1in) wide, to the other two sides. Mark the centre line both ways with basting stitches. Working from the centre outward and using strong thread, oversew the top and bottom edges to the roller tapes. Fit the side pieces into the slots, and roll any extra fabric on one roller until the fabric is taut.

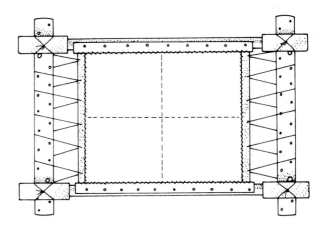

2 Insert the pegs or adjust the screw attachments to secure the frame. Thread a large-eyed needle (chenille needle) with strong thread or fine string and lace both edges, securing the ends around the intersections of the frame. Lace the webbing at 2.5cm (1in) intervals, stretching the fabric evenly.

EXTENDING EMBROIDERY FABRIC

It is easy to extend a piece of embroidery fabric, such as a bookmark, to stretch it in a hoop.

● Fabric oddments of a similar weight can be used. Simply cut four pieces to size (in other words, to the measurement that will fit both the embroidery fabric and your hoop) and baste them to each side of the embroidery fabric before stretching it in the hoop in the usual way.

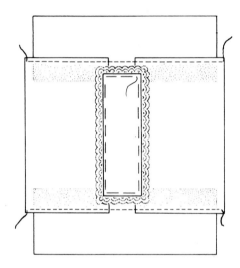

TO MITRE A CORNER

Press a single hem to the wrong side, the same as the measurement given in the instructions. Open the hem out again and fold the corner of the fabric inwards as shown on the diagram. Refold the hem to the wrong side along the pressed line, and slip-stitch in place.

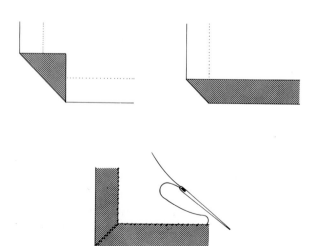

MOUNTING EMBROIDERY

The cardboard should be cut to the size of the finished embroidery, with an extra 6mm (¼in) added all around to allow for the recess in the frame.

LIGHTWEIGHT FABRICS

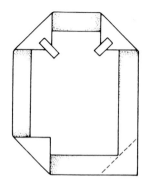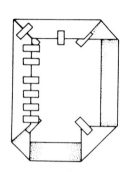

1 Place the embroidery face down, with the cardboard centred on top, and basting and pencil lines matching. Begin by folding over the fabric at each corner and securing it with masking tape.

2 Working first on one side and then the other, fold over the fabric on all sides and secure it firmly with pieces of masking tape, placed about 2.5cm (1in) apart. Also neaten the mitred corners with masking tape, pulling the fabric tightly to give a firm, smooth finish.

HEAVIER FABRICS

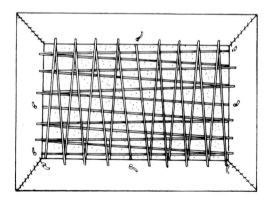

● Lay the embroidery face down, with the cardboard centred on top; fold over the edges of the fabric on opposite sides, making mitred folds at the corners, and lace across, using strong thread. Repeat on the other two sides. Finally, pull up the stitches fairly tightly to stretch the fabric firmly over the cardboard. Overstitch the mitred corners.

MOUNTING A PICTURE IN A FLEXI-LOOP

Cut out a felt backing disc, using the inside of the ring as a template. Stretch the finished embroidery over the inside ring and hold it in place by stretching the outer ring over it. Trim the fabric at the back to within 2.5cm (1in) of the edge and gather together, 12mm (½in) from the edge. Fix the felt disc in place by oversewing round the edge or glue in place with a fabric adhesive.

CROSS STITCH

For all cross stitch embroidery, the following two methods of working are used. In each case, neat rows of vertical stitches are produced on the back of the fabric.

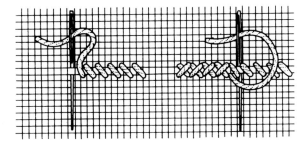

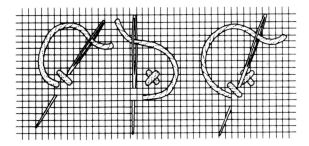

● When stitching large areas, work in horizontal rows. Working from right to left, complete the first row of evenly spaced diagonal stitches over the number of threads specified in the project instructions. Then, working from left to right, repeat the process. Continue in this way, making sure each stitch crosses in the same direction.

● When stitching diagonal lines, work downwards, completing each stitch before moving to the next. When starting a project always begin to embroider at the centre of the design and work outwards to ensure that the design will be placed centrally on the fabric.

FRENCH KNOTS

To work a french knot, bring your needle and cotton out slightly to the right of where you want your knot to be. Wind the thread once around the needle and insert the needle to the left of the point where you brought it out.

Be careful not to pull too hard or the knot will disappear through the fabric.

BACKSTITCH

Backstitch is used in the projects to give emphasis to a particular foldline, an outline or a shadow. The stitches are worked over the same number of threads as the cross stitch, forming continuous straight or diagonal lines.

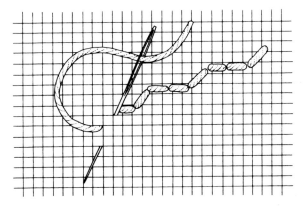

● Make the first stitch from left to right; pass the needle behind the fabric and bring it out one stitch length ahead to the left. Repeat and continue in this way along the line.

ADDING NAMES AND DATES TO A SAMPLER

First of all, on graph paper, draw your names and dates, using your chosen alphabet. Count the number of stitches in the width of the name or date and mark the centre, then draw the names and dates again, matching the centres with the centre of the sampler.

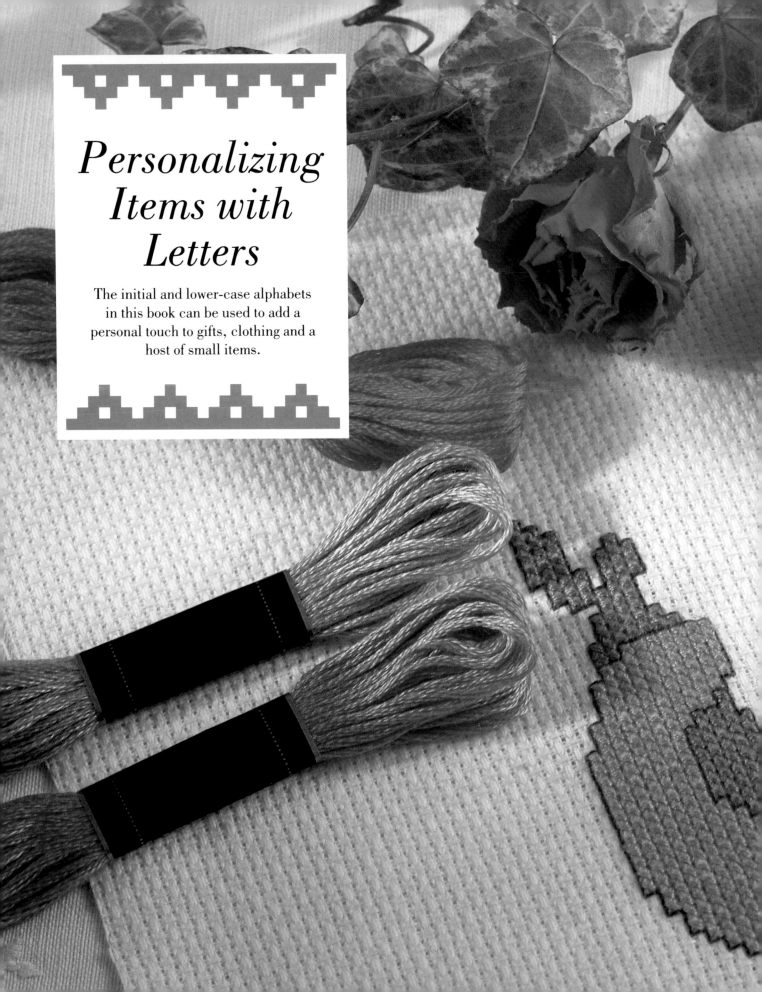

Personalizing Items with Letters

The initial and lower-case alphabets in this book can be used to add a personal touch to gifts, clothing and a host of small items.

PERSONALIZING ITEMS WITH LETTERS

The letters which we use today to communicate had their origins in prehistoric times. Primitive people carved or painted pictures on the walls of their caves to tell a story. Gradually the pictures changed and began to stand for words rather than objects and thus began the first alphabets. The influence of the Egyptians, Phoenicians, Greeks and Romans all contributed towards the alphabet with which we are familiar today.

Letters varied in style and design according to which tools they were written with. A quill, for example, produced lettering which was curved and ornamental.

In the 5th century the Irish monks wrote the Book of Kells. This beautifully illuminated manuscript, each page of which features an elaborate initial in the curving Celtic style, intertwined with mythical beasts and strange flowers and foliage, is an excellent example of how beautiful decorative lettering can be.

Through the centuries, lettering changed dramatically. Even the type of material on which the lettering was written made a great difference to the style of writing. Wood and metal were common materials, and whilst wood produced a soft flowing style of writing, engraving on metal created a more angular form of lettering.

In the 15th century printing was invented and to a certain extent the art of calligraphy was lost. Fortunately, the styles of printing are reverting back to the original type faces used by the first printers, which were more attractive than some of the more modern styles.

Lettering and monograms have been used in embroidery for hundreds of years. Some of the early samplers provided a record of children's lives and showed a skill in needlework from a very early age. These early samplers were worked in cross stitch on a fine evenweave linen and the lettering was enhanced with patterns and borders.

Monograms are an effective way of decorating personal possessions such as book covers, cushions and boxes. Highly decorative letters can make a beautiful finished design in themselves.

THE ALPHABETS

In this book, you will find many ways to use letters. With the Animal alphabet, you can add a touch of individuality to clothes, using the waste canvas technique (see page 22) to transfer the design. Dungarees, jumpers, blouses and dresses can be all transformed into unique garments in no time at all.

By using a lower case alphabet you can sew your child's name and make it into a picture for the nursery or just embroider and frame an initial. A card or bib on the birth of a baby can make a happy occasion extra special.

The Wreath alphabet has a multitude of uses. The strawberry and berry wreaths would be suitable for decorating a kitchen – perhaps in the form of small framed letters, or embroidered on oven gloves or a tea cosy – while the floral wreaths might be used for boxes, pincushions or napkins, as well as the ideas in this book. Any letters can be used in the wreath of your choice, as all the letters are designed to fit into any of the wreaths.

The ornate letters of the Romantic alphabet have been worked in subtle shades for a dainty feel to the embroidery. For those who prefer brighter colours, the alphabet would look equally attractive worked in strong shades of cotton.

CHANGING THE SIZE OF A LETTER

If a letter will be over large for a particular frame or card, the easiest way to adjust the size is to change the fabric. Evenweave fabrics are graded according to their 'count', which is the number of intersections per 2.5cm (1in). A 12-count Aida fabric, therefore, has 12 Aida blocks per 12.5cm (1in), each stitch being taken over one block, whereas an 18-count Aida will have 18 blocks per 2.5cm (1in). This means that a row of, say, 30 stitches will cover 6.5cm (2½in) of 12-count Aida, but only about 4.5cm (1¾in) of the latter.

Other evenweave fabrics, such as Hardanger, may have a higher count, but in the case of a fabric with a high count each cross stitch is normally worked over two fabric threads. A 26-count even-

weave, therefore, will normally have 13 stitches per 2.5cm (1in).

To work out how large a letter will be on varying fabrics, therefore, you must first count the maximum number of stitches from side to side, and from the top to the bottom. Divide each number by the number of stitches that you will make per 2.5cm (1in) on your intended material. If the letter will be too large, change to a fabric with a higher count, and vice versa.

For example, assuming that your chosen letter is a maximum of 38 stitches high and 11 stitches across: divide 38 (the number of stitches) by 14 (the count of the fabric) to reach 2.7.

The initial will be 2.7 × 2.5cm/1in = 6.75cm (2¾in) high and, using the same method, just under 2cm (or ¾in) across. If it is to fit into a frame just 5cm (2in) high, it will obviously be neccessary to use a fabric with a higher count.

To embroider a full name, use the alphabet below, or one of those on pages 46-7, to complete the name.

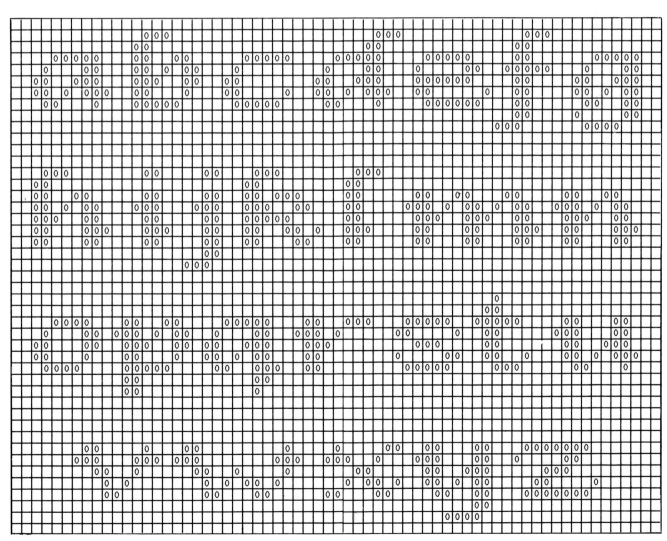

Romantic Alphabet

This lovely alphabet would be ideal for enhancing wedding gifts. A card and bookmark might include the initials of both the bride and groom, while guests' initials might decorate placecards.

ROMANTIC ALPHABET

YOU WILL NEED

For the Card, measuring 9cm × 12cm
(3½in × 4¾in), with an aperture measuring
5.5cm × 7cm (2¼in × 2¾in):

*10cm (4in) square of 26-count, white evenweave
fabric
Stranded embroidery cotton in the colours given in
the panel
No26 tapestry needle
Card, for suppliers see page 48*

For the Gift tag, measuring 7cm × 5cm
(2¾in × 2in), with an aperture measuring
4cm (1½in) in diameter:

*10cm (4in) square of 18-count, white Aida fabric
Stranded embroidery cotton in the colours given
in the panel
No26 tapestry needle
Gift tag, for suppliers see page 48*

For the Bookmark, measuring 9cm × 20.5cm
(3½in × 8¼in), including the lace edging:

*Stranded embroidery cotton in the colours given
in the panel
No26 tapestry needle
18-count Aida bookmark, for suppliers see page 48*

For the Initial in an oval frame, measuring
5.5cm × 7cm (2¼in × 2¾in), with an aperture
measuring 4.5cm × 6cm (1¾in × 2⅜in):

*10cm × 15cm (4in × 6in) of 14-count, cream
Aida fabric
Stranded embroidery cotton in the colours given
in the panel
No24 tapestry needle
Oval frame, for suppliers see page 48*

For the Miniature framed initial, measuring
6.5cm (2½in) in diameter, with an aperture
measuring 5cm (2in) in diameter:

*8cm (3¼in) square of 18-count, cream Aida fabric
Stranded embroidery cotton in the colours given
in the panel
No26 tapestry needle
Miniature metal frame, for suppliers see page 48*

For the Napkin, measuring 40cm (16in) square:

*Stranded embroidery cotton in the colours given
in the panel
No24 tapestry needle
Ready-prepared ivory napkin, for suppliers see
page 48*

•

THE CARD

Prepare the fabric and mark the centre with horizontal and vertical lines of basting stitches. Mount it in a hoop as explained on page 4. Start the stitching at the centre, using two strands of cotton in the needle. Work each stitch over two fabric threads in each direction. Make sure that all the top crosses run in the same direction and that each row is worked into the same holes as the top and bottom of the row before, so that you do not leave a space between the rows.

MAKING UP

Gently steam press the embroidery on the wrong side and trim to within 12mm (½in) larger than the aperture. Centre your embroidery behind the opening and secure in place with double-sided tape.
  Press the card firmly together.

THE GIFT TAG

This is made in the same way as the card, but you will have to use 18-count fabric for the embroidery.

THE BOOKMARK

Mark the centre of the bookmark from top to bottom with a line of basting stitches. Measure 4cm (1½in) up from the bottom of the bookmark and make another line of basting stitches. This will show you where to place the centre of your letter.
  Start the stitching at the centre, using one strand of cotton in the needle. Work each stitch over one block of fabric in each direction. Make sure that all the top crosses run in the same direction, and that each row is worked into the same holes as the top or bottom of the row before, so that you do not leave a space between the rows. Gently steam press the finished embroidery on the wrong side.

INITIAL IN AN OVAL FRAME

Prepare the fabric and mark the centre with horizontal and vertical lines of basting stitches. Mount it in a hoop as explained on page 4.

Start the stitching at the centre, using two strands of cotton in the needle. Work each stitch over one block of fabric in each direction. Make sure that all the top crosses run in the same direction and that each row is worked into the same holes as the top or bottom of the row before, so that you do not leave a space between the rows.

MAKING UP

Gently steam press the embroidery on the wrong side. Using the white plastic back of the frame as a guide, place the embroidery centrally over the back and trim around the edge. Place the acetate front and embroidery face down in the frame and secure by clicking the back in place.

MINIATURE FRAMED INITIAL

Prepare the fabric and mark the centre with horizontal and vertical lines of basting stitches. Mount it in a hoop as explained on page 4. Start the stitching at the centre, using one strand of cotton in the needle. Work each stitch over one block of fabric in each direction. Make sure that all the top crosses run in the same direction and that each row is worked into the same holes as the top or bottom of the row before, so that you do not leave a space between the rows.

MAKING UP

Gently steam press the embroidery on the wrong side. Using the cream backing paper from the frame as a guide, place the embroidery centrally on the top and trim around the edge. Place the acetate, embroidery and cardboard disc face down in the frame and secure with the felt adhesive disc.

THE NAPKIN

Measure 4cm (1½in) vertically up from the bottom right hand corner and 4cm (1½in) horizontally in from the right-hand side and sew horizontal and vertical lines of basting stitches. The point at which they cross is the centre of the letter. Mount the napkin in a hoop as explained on page 4. Start the stitching at the centre of the chosen initial, using two strands of cotton in the needle. Work each stitch over two threads of fabric in each direction. Make sure that all the top crosses run in the same direction and that each row is worked into the same holes as the top or bottom of the row before, so that you do not leave a space between the rows. Gently steam press the embroidery on the wrong side.

ROMANTIC ALPHABET		DMC	ANCHOR	MADEIRA
X	Yellow	3078	292	0102
–	Light pink	3689	66	0606
<	Dark pink	3688	68	0605
=	Green	471	265	1502
Z	Grey	415	398	1803
	Dark green*	3345	268	1406

Note: for bks outline use one strand of dark green* (used for bks only).

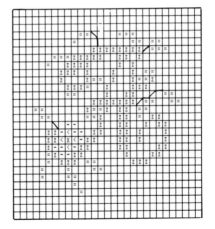

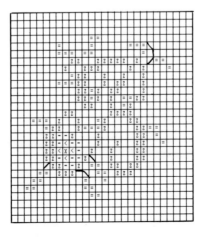

Turn to page 18 for charts for the remaining letters. 15

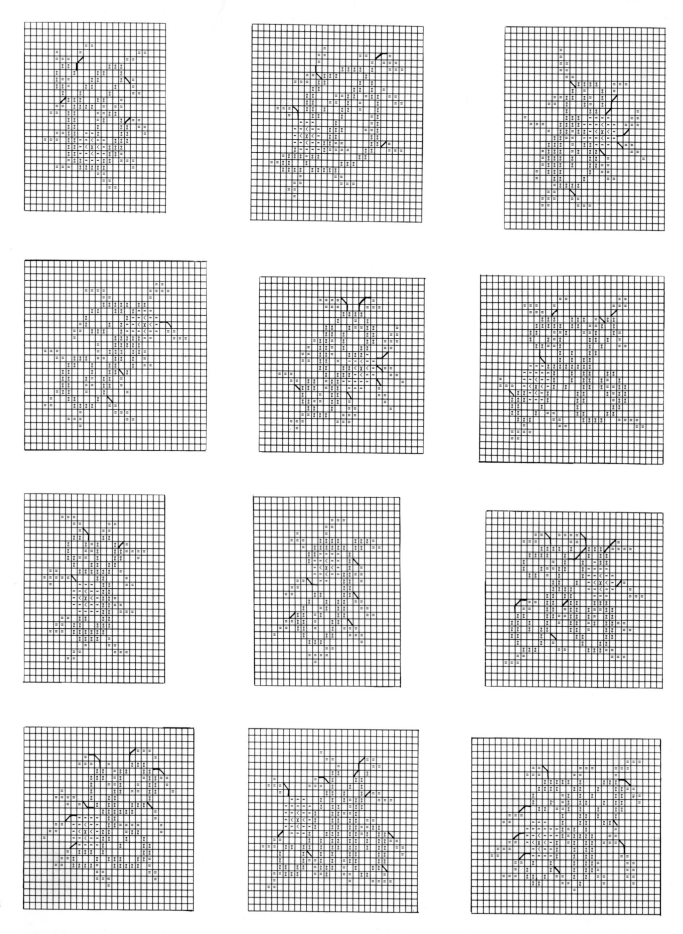

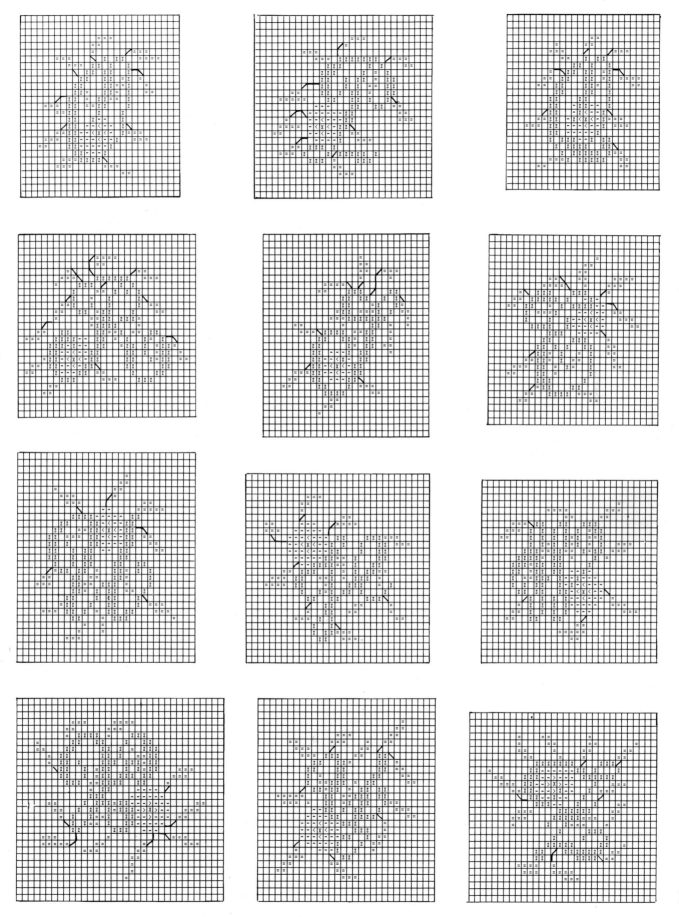

Animal Alphabet

These striking designs would bring a smile to the face of any child. Take your child's initial and either embroider this on its own or combine it with letters from a lower case alphabet (see pages 46-7) to make the full name.

ANIMAL ALPHABET

YOU WILL NEED

For the Card, measuring 20cm × 15cm
(8in × 6in), with an oval aperture measuring
15cm × 10cm (6in × 4in):

*25cm × 20cm (10in × 8in) of 14-count, white
Aida fabric
Stranded embroidery cotton in the colours given
in the panel
No24 tapestry needle
Card, for suppliers see page 48*

For the Framed Initial, here in a frame measuring
15cm × 11.5cm (6in × 4½in), with an aperture
measuring 13cm × 10cm (5¼in × 4in):

*20cm × 15cm (8in × 6in) of 14-count, white
Aida fabric
Stranded embroidery cotton in the colours given
in the panel
No24 tapestry needle
Frame of your choice*

*NOTE: the letters vary in size, and the embroidery
for both the card and the picture can be worked on
virtually any count of evenweave fabric.
To calculate the dimensions of your chosen
initial(s), and perhaps change to fabric of a higher
or lower count, refer to pages 40-43.*

For the Bib, measuring 18.5cm × 15cm
(7⅜in × 6in):

*Stranded embroidery cotton in the colours given
in the panel
No24 tapestry needle
Evenweave bib, for suppliers see page 48*

To embroider initials on purchased
(non-evenweave) clothes:

*Stranded embroidery cotton in the colours given
in the panel
No24 tapestry needle
Zweigart's waste canvas, with 14 threads per
2.5cm (1in), a piece 5cm (2in) larger each way
than the dimensions of the finished
embroidered initial
Fine tweezers
Water spray
Basting cotton and needle
Chosen item of clothing*

THE CARD

Prepare the fabric, marking the centre with horizontal and vertical lines of basting stitches. Mount it in a hoop as explained on page 4. Start the stitching at the centre, using two strands of cotton in the needle, if using 14-count Aida (see Stitching details). Take each stitch over one block of fabric in each direction, making sure that all the top crosses run in the same direction and that each row is worked into the same holes as the top or bottom of the row before, so that you do not leave a space between rows.

MAKING UP

Gently steam press the embroidery on the wrong side and trim it to measure 12mm (½in) larger each way than the aperture. Centre your embroidery behind the opening and secure it in place with double-sided tape. Press the card firmly together.

THE FRAMED INITIAL

The embroidery is worked in the same way as for the card. Gently steam press the finished embroidery on the wrong side; mount it (see page 6), and set it in a frame of your choice.

THE BIB

Mark the centre of the bib with horizontal and vertical lines of basting stitches, and embroider your chosen initial (see individual stitching details), using two strands of embroidery cotton in the needle and taking each stitch over one block of the fabric.

When you have finished, remove the basting stitches and gently steam press the bib on the wrong side.

USING WASTE CANVAS

Position the blue threads of the canvas horizontally or vertically with the weave of the garment. Pin and then baste the canvas in place and remove the pins. Each pair of canvas threads is treated as one thread, so the cross stitch is worked over one pair of threads in each direction. Start stitching in the centre, which you can mark on the canvas with a vertical and horizontal line of basting stitches. Begin the embroidery by fastening the cotton with your first stitches, and finish by threading the cotton through a few stitches at the back of the work. Make sure that you start and finish firmly, so that the stitches do not pull out during washing.

When the cross stitching is complete, trim the

canvas to within 12mm (½in) of the embroidery. Dampen the embroidery on the right side with warm water and leave for a few minutes until the threads soften. Using tweezers, pull the canvas threads out one at a time so that you do not damage your embroidery.

Press the embroidery by placing it right side down on a towel and pressing with a hot iron and damp cloth.

ALPHABET STITCHING DETAILS

All letters are worked using three strands of stranded cotton for 11-count fabric, two for 14-count fabric and one for 18- or 22-count fabric.

All outlining is in backstitch, using one strand of dark grey unless stated otherwise. Additional stitching details are as follows:

The letter B
Embroider the bee's wings in backstitch with one strand of dark grey.

The letter C
Embroider the whiskers in backstitch with two strands of black cotton.

The letters E and J
Embroider the water in backstitch with two strands of dark blue.

The letter I
Embroider the feelers in backstitch, using two strands of black cotton.

The letter L
Embroider the feelers in backstitch, using two strands of black cotton.

The letter R
Embroider the whiskers in backstitch with one strand of dark grey cotton.

The letter S
Embroider the whiskers in straight stitch with one strand of black cotton.

The letter U
Embroider the tufts of hair in backstitch with two strands of yellow cotton.

The letter V
Embroider the vipers' tongue in backstitch, using two strands of black cotton.

The letter W
Embroider the water in backstitch with two strands of pale blue.

ANIMAL ALPHABET		DMC	ANCHOR	MADEIRA
C	Light gold	676	887	2208
V	Dark gold	729	890	2209
/	Light brown	437	362	2011
=	Medium brown	435	(363)	2009
Z	Dark brown	434	365	2008
X	Moss green	471	265	(1501)
S	Light jade green	563	208	1207
W	Dark jade green	562	210	(1206)
r	Red	349	(46)	0212
.	Yellow	743	301	0109
e	Light blue	800	128	1014
n	Dark blue	799	130	1012
+	Light grey	318	235	1802
>	Medium grey	414	399	1801
−	Pink	604	60	(0614)
a	Mauve	340	118	0902
*	Black	Black	403	Black
0	White	White	1	White
	Dark grey*	3799	(236)	(1713)

Note: numbers in brackets indicate the nearest colour match; for bks outline use dark grey* (used for bks only).

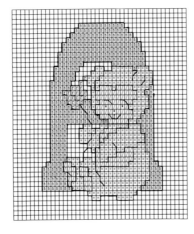

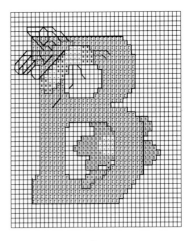

Turn to page 26 for charts for the remaining letters.

23

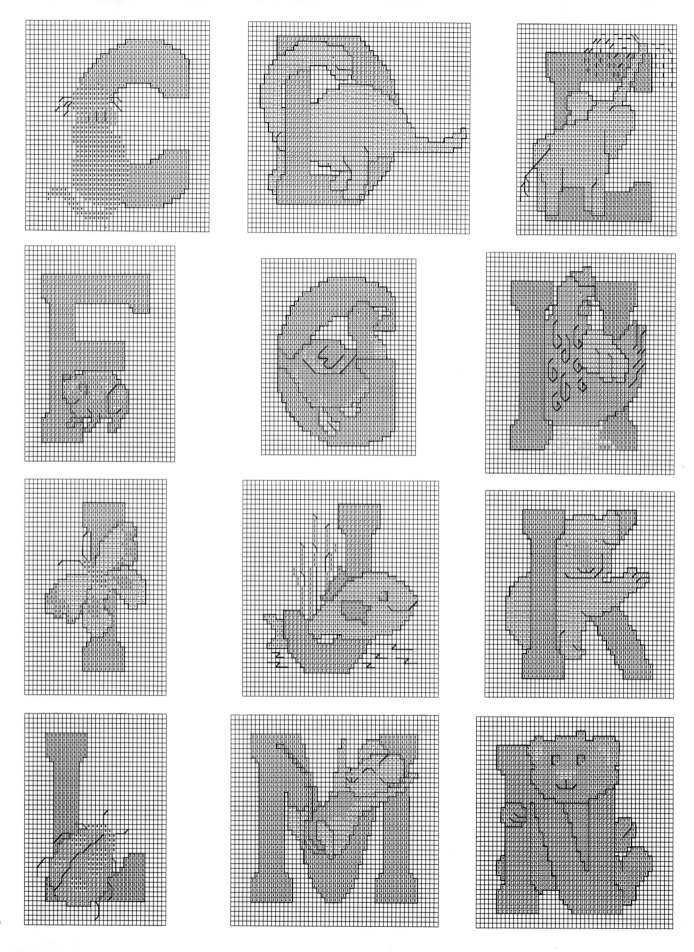

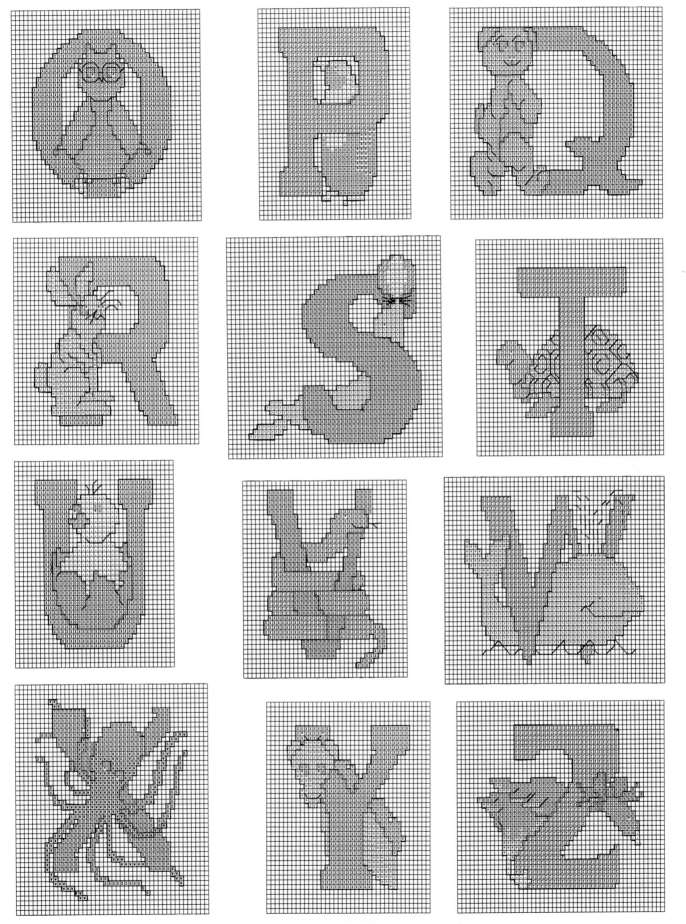

Wreath Alphabet

Charming wreaths of flowers or fruits make a highly versatile alphabet. The paperweight or the box with a rosebud wreath would grace any lounge, while the fruit garland might encircle covers for homemade jams and preserves.

WREATH ALPHABET

YOU WILL NEED

For the Paperweight, measuring 6.5cm (2½in) in diameter:

*10cm (4in) square of white, 18-count Aida fabric
Stranded embroidery cotton in the colours given in the panel
No26 tapestry needle*

For the Porcelain box, with a lid measuring 9cm (3½in) in diameter:

*13cm (5¼in) square of cream, 14-count Aida fabric
Stranded embroidery cotton in the colours given in the panel
No24 tapestry needle*

For each Jam-pot cover, measuring 15.5cm (6¼in) in diameter, with a central circle of 18-count Aida fabric, measuring 6.5cm (2½in) in diameter:

*Ready-prepared cover, for suppliers, see page 48
70cm (28in) of matching ribbon, 6mm (¼in) wide
Stranded embroidery cotton in the colours given in the panel
No26 tapestry needle*

For the Card, measuring 13cm × 16.5cm (5¼in × 6½in), with an aperture measuring 9.5cm (3¾in):

*15cm (6in) square of white, 14-count Aida fabric
Stranded embroidery cotton in the colours given in the panel
No24 tapestry needle
Purchased card, for suppliers, see page 48*

For the Pot-pourri pillow, measuring 25cm (10in) square, excluding the lace edging:

*27.5cm (11in) square of white Schonfells fabric, with a 12-count centre, 9.5cm (3¾in) in diameter
27.5cm (11in) square of white cotton fabric
2.4m (2¾yds) of lace edging, 4cm (1½in) wide
Polyester filling
Pot-pourri sachet
Stranded embroidery cotton in the colours given in the panel
No24 tapestry needle
White sewing cotton and needle*

THE PAPERWEIGHT

Prepare the fabric and mark the centre with horizontal and vertical lines of basting stitches. Mount it in a hoop as explained on page 4. Start the stitching at the centre, using one strand of embroidery cotton in the needle. Work each stitch over one block of fabric in each direction. Make sure that all the top crosses run in the same direction and that the top or bottom of each row is worked into the same holes as the row before, so that you do not leave a space between the rows.

Outline the flowers with one strand of dark green cotton.

MAKING UP

Centre the finished embroidery on the cream backing paper provided with the paperweight, using the basting lines as a guide. Trim the fabric carefully to the size of the paper. Remove basting stitches and place the embroidery and paper face downwards in the recess at the bottom of the paperweight; secure both with the adhesive felt backing disc.

THE BOX

Prepare the fabric and mark the centre with horizontal and vertical lines of basting stitches. Mount it in a hoop as explained on page 4. Start the stitching at the centre, using two strands of cotton in the needle. Work each stitch over one block of fabric in each direction. Make sure that all the top crosses run in the same direction and that the top or bottom of each row is worked into the same holes as the row before so that you do not leave a space between the rows. Outline flowers and embroider stalks in backstitch, using one strand of dark green cotton.

Gently steam press the embroidery on the wrong side. Use the basting stitches as a guide to centre the design, removing them when you have trimmed the fabric. Follow the manufacturer's instructions for assembling the lid.

JAM-POT COVERS

For each cover, prepare the fabric and mark the centre with horizontal and vertical lines of basting stitches. Mount it in a hoop as explained on page 4. Start the stitching at the centre, using one strand of embroidery cotton in the needle. Take each stitch over one block of fabric in each direction. Make sure that all the top crosses run in the same direction and that the top or bottom of each row is worked into the same holes as the row before so that you do not leave a space between the rows.

Outline the flowers and berries and work the stalks in backstitch, using one strand of dark green cotton in the needle. The seeds on the strawberries are worked with cream french knots (see page 7). Tie the finished cover to your jar with a matching length of coloured ribbon.

THE CARD

Prepare the fabric and mark the centre with horizontal and vertical lines of basting stitches. Mount it in a hoop as explained on page 4. Start the stitching at the centre, using two strands of embroidery cotton in the needle. Work each stitch over one block of fabric in each direction. Make sure that all the top crosses run in the same direction and that each row is worked into the same holes as the top or bottom of the row before, so that you do not leave a space between the rows.

Outline the flowers and embroider the stalks in backstitch, using one strand of dark green cotton in the needle.

MAKING UP

Gently steam press the embroidery on the wrong side and trim to measure 12mm (½in) larger each way than the aperture. Centre your embroidery behind the opening and secure it in place with double-sided tape. Press the card firmly together.

POT-POURRI PILLOW

Prepare the fabric and mark the centre with horizontal and vertical lines of basting stitches. Mount the fabric in a frame or hoop as explained on page 4. Start the stitching at the centre, using three strands of embroidery cotton in the needle. Work each stitch over one block of fabric in each direction. Make sure that all the top crosses run in the same direction and that each row is worked into the same holes as the top or bottom of the row before, so that you do not leave a space between the rows.

Work the stalks in backstitch, with one strand of dark green cotton in the needle.

MAKING UP

Gently steam press the work on the wrong side. Join the edges of the lace together with a small french seam and run a gathering thread along the edge of the lace. Pull the gathers up to fit around the edge of the pillow and, with right sides together and the lace lying on the fabric with the decorative edge facing inwards, baste the lace to the edge of the embroidery, just inside the 12mm (½in) seam allowance. Spread the gathers evenly, allowing the extra fullness at the corners, and machine stitch in place. Place the backing fabric on top, right sides together; baste, and then machine stitch in place, taking a 12mm (½in) seam allowance and leaving a 20cm (8in) opening along one side. Remove basting stitches; trim across the corners, and turn the pillow cover right side out. Fill with loose polyester wadding and the pot-pourri sachet; slipstitch the opening.

WREATH ALPHABET		DMC	ANCHOR	MADEIRA
–	Light mauve	208	111	0804
S	Dark mauve	550	101	0714
Z	Pink	3689	66	0606
r	Crimson	3608	86	0709
X	Light moss green	3052	844	1509
=	Dark moss green	3051	845	1508
0	Bright green	3348	264	1409
.	Cream	746	275	0101
e	Yellow	743	301	0113
V	Light blue	800	128	0909
+	Dark blue	799	130	0910
n	Light red	349	12	0212
C	Dark red	304	47	0513
/	Brown	640	393	1905

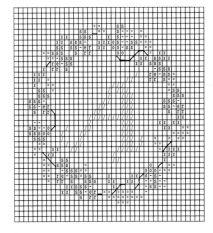

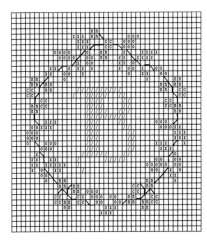

Turn to page 34 for charts for the remaining letters.

31

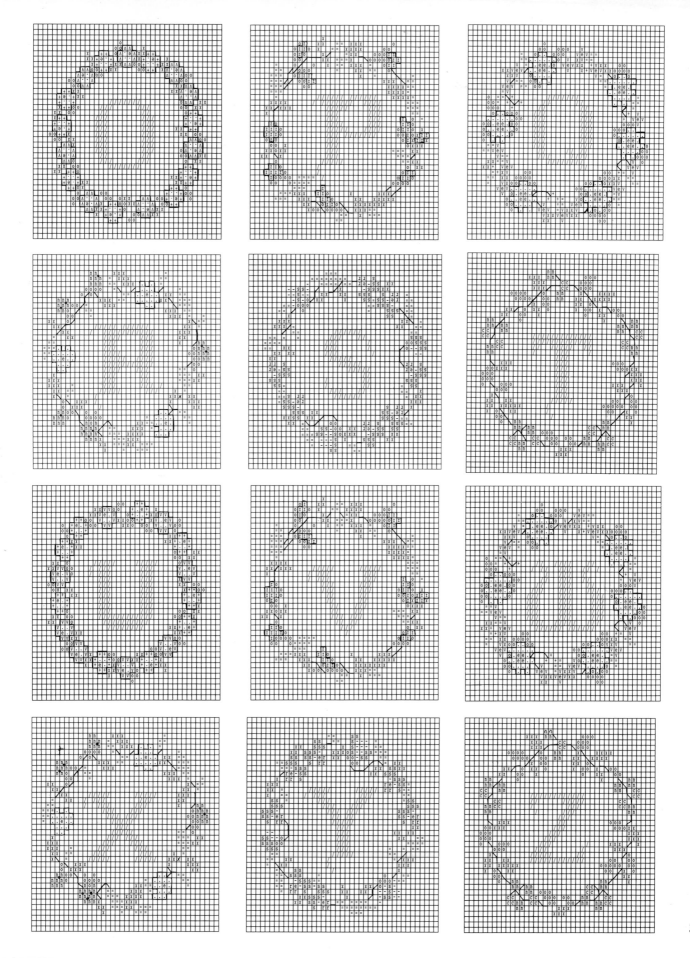

Traditional Alphabet Sampler

Letters and patterns such as these adorned the parlours of Victorian ladies. This simplified version is designed to bring a traditional air to a room setting.

TRADITIONAL ALPHABET SAMPLER

YOU WILL NEED

For the Traditional Alphabet sampler, with a design area measuring 24cm × 17cm (9½in × 6¾in) or 137 stitches by 96 stitches, here in a frame measuring 34cm × 27cm (13½in × 10¾in):

35cm × 28cm (14¼ × 11½in) of beige, 28-count Quaker cloth
Stranded embroidery cotton in the colours given in the panel
No 24 tapestry needle
Strong thread for lacing across the back
Cardboard for mounting, sufficient to fit into frame recess
Frame of your choice

●

THE EMBROIDERY

Prepare the fabric, and baste horizontal and vertical centre lines (see page 4). Stretch the fabric in a frame, as explained on page 5. Following the chart, start the embroidery at the centre of the design, using two strands of embroidery cotton in the needle. Work each stitch over two threads of fabric in each direction. Make sure that all the top crosses run in the same direction and that each row is worked into the same holes as the top or bottom of the row before, so that you do not leave a space between the rows.

MAKING UP

Gently steam press the work on the wrong side and mount it as explained on page 6. To retain the traditional feel of the sampler, choose a simple wooden frame without a cardboard mount.

TRADITIONAL ALPHABET ▶		DMC	ANCHOR	MADEIRA
V	Gold	834	874	2204
X	Dark blue	930	922	(1712)
=	Light blue	931	921	(1711)
S	Dark brown	3790	905	2003
r	Light brown	640	393	1905
0	Dark green	3362	263	1601
–	Light green	3052	844	1509
e	Dark peach	922	337	0310
+	Light peach	402	347	2307

Modern Alphabet Sampler

This alphabet, with its subtle combination of greens, greys and mauves, would fit easily into most modern colour schemes. Choose a mount to enhance your own particular decor.

MODERN ALPHABET SAMPLER

YOU WILL NEED

For the Modern Alphabet sampler, with a design area measuring 18.5cm × 25.5cm (7¼in × 10¼in), or 101 stitches by 155 stitches, here in a frame measuring 32cm × 39cm (12¾in × 15½in):

30cm × 37cm (12in × 14¾in) of white, 14-count Aida fabric
Stranded embroidery cotton in the colours given in the panel
No 24 tapestry needle
Strong thread for lacing across the back
Cardboard for mounting, sufficient to fit into the frame recess
Frame of your choice

●

THE EMBROIDERY

Prepare the fabric, marking the centre with horizontal and vertical lines of basting stitches, and stretch it in a frame as explained on page 5. Following the chart, start the embroidery at the centre of the design, using two strands of embroidery cotton in the needle. Work each stitch over one block of fabric in each direction. Make sure that all the top crosses run in the same direction and that each row is worked into the same holes as the top or bottom of the row before, so that you do not leave a space between the rows.

MAKING UP

Gently steam press the finished embroidery on the wrong side and mount it as explained on page 6. Choose a suitably modern frame to display your sampler.

MODERN ALPHABET ▶		DMC	ANCHOR	MADEIRA
–	Dark mauve	208	111	0804
S	Light mauve	211	342	0801
V	Dark grey	415	398	1803
=	Light grey	762	234	1804
0	Dark green	367	216	1312
X	Light green	368	214	1310

Note: for backstitch lines use one strand of dark green.

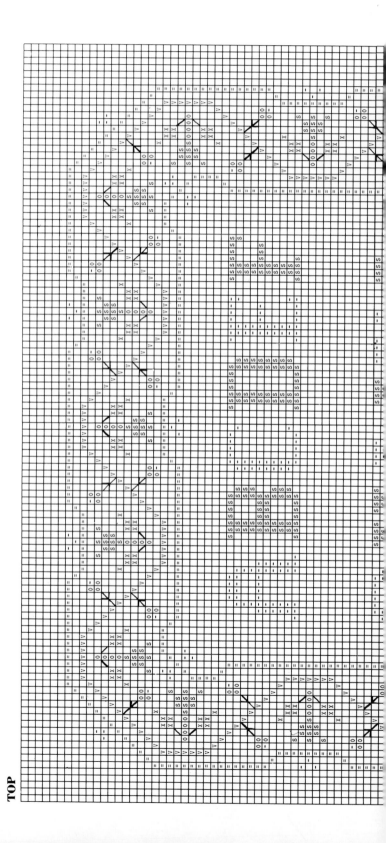

TOP

Lower-case Alphabets

Sometimes you may want to stitch a full name or a message, rather than just an initial. Here is a choice of cross stitch alphabets designed to go with the more elaborate initials of the previous pages.

LOWER-CASE
ALPHABETS

To use these alphabets, it is necessary first to work out the spacing on graph paper (see page 7). These alphabets are designed to be used with any of the capital / initial alphabets given in this book, and can be stitched in whichever colour is appropriate for your particular project.

The lower-case cross stitch alphabets given here would be ideal for many purposes – adding a name to the centre of a sampler, for example. There are other cases, however, where the cross stitch lettering would be too large and cumbersome; for example, you might wish to make a Valentine's Day card with a verse of poetry, starting with an elaborate cross stitch initial from the Romantic alphabet. In this case, it would be better to 'write' the words in backstitch lettering, perhaps in an italic effect.

To do this, take a sheet of graph paper and a pencil and first draw out the initial, as shown here. Next, write out the rest of the verse, using your chosen handwriting. Go over the writing again, remembering that each backstitch must be indicated by a line either running from corner to corner of a square or horizontally (see the backstitching of the Animal alphabet).

When you are making your backstitch chart, remember that the scale will be the same as that of the charted initial. If you are not sure about the stitched size, make a small sample of the lettering on your chosen fabric before stitching the main project.

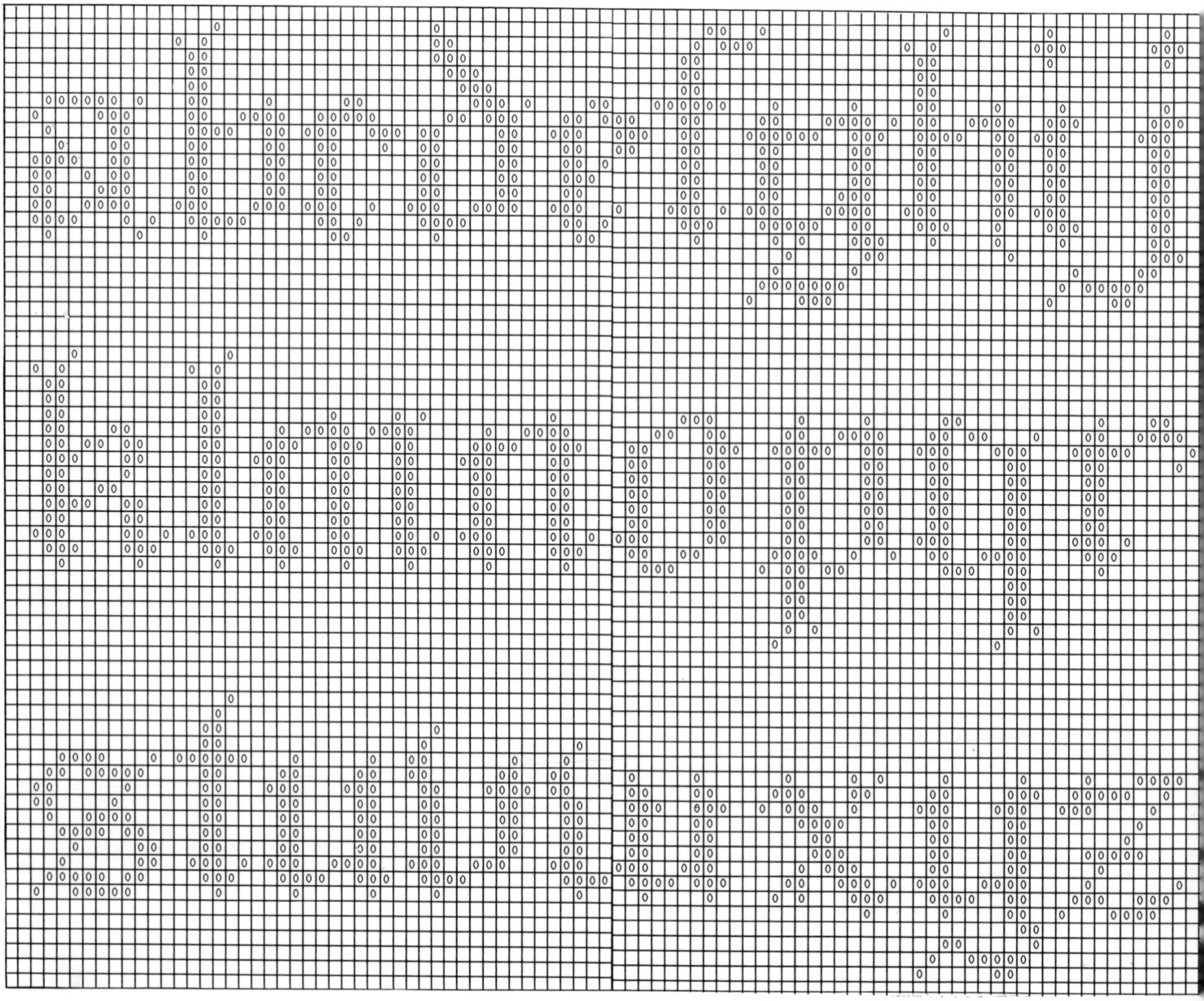

46

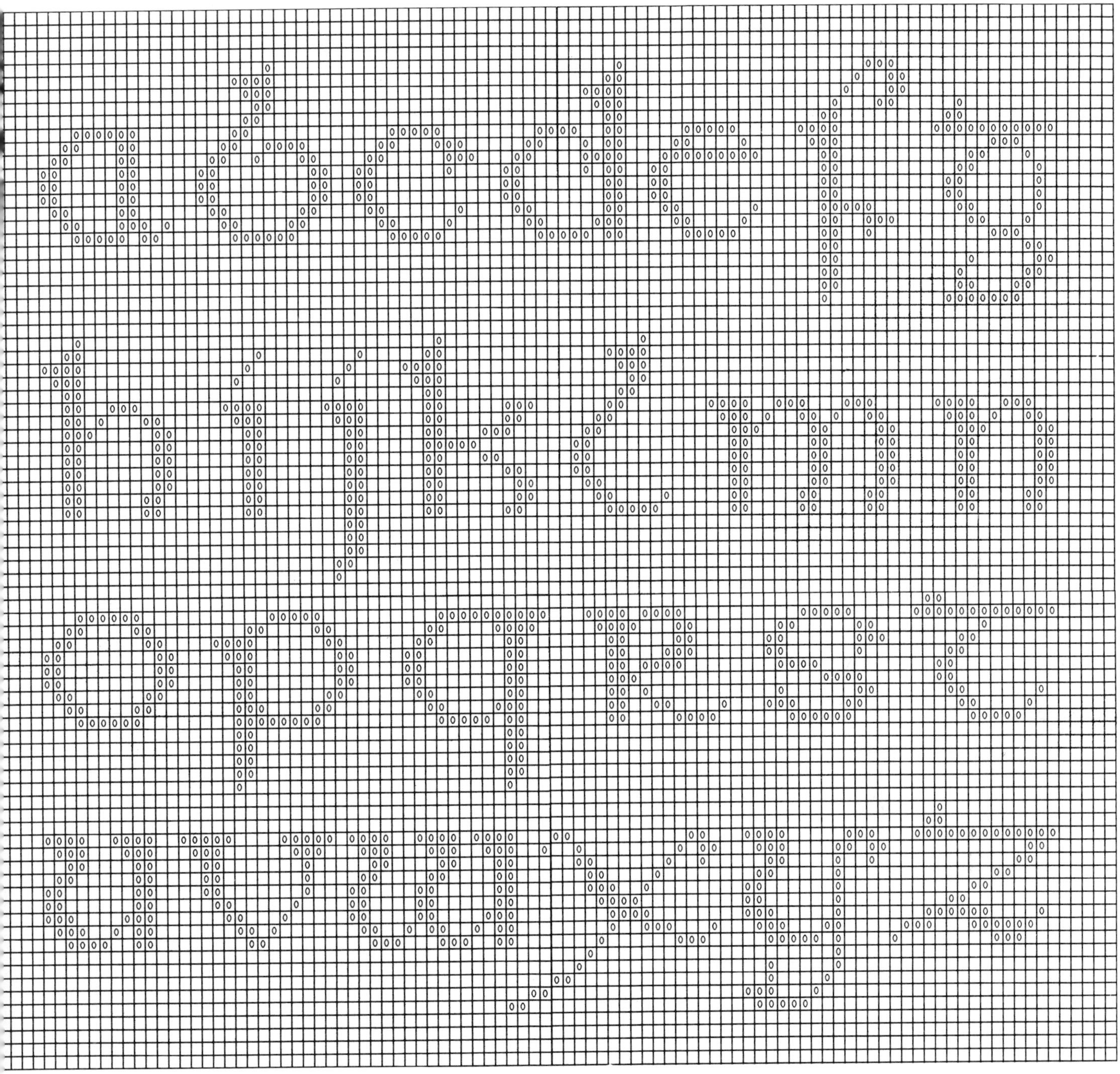

ACKNOWLEDGEMENTS

The Author would like to
thank the following people for their help with this book:

Helen Burke, Kate Riley and Diane Teal.
Thanks are also due to DMC Creative World Ltd for
supplying fabrics and threads and Framecraft
Miniatures Ltd for supplying the paperweight, porcelain
box, jar covers, frames, bookmark and serviette.
Both suppliers request that a stamped self-addressed
envelope be enclosed with all enquiries.

The baby's bib was supplied by:
Crafty Ideas, 'The Willows', Cassington Road,
Eynsham, Witney, Oxon OX8 1LF.

Enquiries about embroidery kits designed by Jane
Alford under the Reflexions and Cross Purposes label
may be sent to: Richard and Jane Alford, Refexions/
Cross Purposes, The Stables, Black Bull Yard, Welton,
Lincoln LN2 3HZ.

SUPPLIERS

The following mail order
company has supplied
some of the basic items
needed for making up the
projects in this book:

Framecraft Miniatures Limited
372/376 Summer Lane
Hockley
Birmingham, B19 3QA
England
Telephone (021) 359 4442

Addresses for Framecraft
stockists worldwide
Ireland Needlecraft Pty. Ltd.
2-4 Keppel Drive
Hallam, Victoria 3803
Australia

Danish Art Needlework
PO Box 442, Lethbridge
Alberta T1J 3Z1
Canada

Sanyei Imports
PO Box 5, Hashima Shi
Gifu 501-62
Japan

The Embroidery Shop
286 Queen Street
Masterton
New Zealand

Anne Brinkley Designs Inc.
246 Walnut Street
Newton
Mass. 02160
USA

S A Threads and Cottons Ltd.
43 Somerset Road
Cape Town
South Africa

For information on your
nearest stockist of
embroidery cotton,
contact the following:

DMC

UK
DMC Creative World Limited
62 Pullman Road
Wigston
Leicester, LE8 2DY
Telephone: 0533 811040

USA
The DMC Corporation
Port Kearney Bld.
10 South Kearney
N.J. 07032-0650
Telephone: 201 589 0606

AUSTRALIA
DMC Needlecraft Pty
P.O. Box 317
Earlswood 2206
NSW 2204
Telephone: 02599 3088

COATS AND ANCHOR

UK
Kilncraigs Mill
Alloa
Clackmannanshire
Scotland, FK10 1EG
Telephone: 0259 723431

USA
Coats & Clark
P.O. Box 27067
Dept CO1
Greenville
SC 29616
Telephone: 803 234 0103

AUSTRALIA
Coats Patons Crafts
Thistle Street
Launceston
Tasmania 7250
Telephone: 00344 4222

MADEIRA

UK
Madeira Threads (UK) Limited
Thirsk Industrial Park
York Road, Thirsk
N. Yorkshire, YO7 3BX
Telephone: 0845 524880

USA
Madeira Marketing Limited
600 East 9th Street
Michigan City
IN 46360
Telephone: 219 873 1000

AUSTRALIA
Penguin Threads Pty Limited
25-27 Izett Street
Prahran
Victoria 3181
Telephone: 03529 4400